Jesus Teac
How to be Wise

Sinclair Ferguson

**This series looks at the teachings of Jesus.
Read the story and discuss the pictures.**

Illustrated by Jeff Anderson

**Published by Christian Focus Publications, Geanies House, Fearn,
Tain, Ross-shire, IV20 1TW, Scotland.**
© **Copyright 2004 Sinclair Ferguson**
www.christianfocus.com **Printed in the United Kingdom**

We usually think that to be wise you need to be old. Sometimes we think that wise people all have grey hair and spectacles.

It is true that some old people are wise.

They have thought about everything that has happened to them.

They see how things work best.
That's what it means to be wise:
to know how to get things to work
for the best.

But Jesus can help us to be wise long before we're old. He shows us how in five lessons that he teaches us.

Lesson One: Don't talk or act as though you know everything. You will end up trying to put everyone right. You will not notice that there are wrong things in your own life.

People who always complain about others don't see their own faults. Deal with your own faults then you are able to help others.

Lesson Two: Some people don't see any faults in others. That's not wise either. Jesus said something like this: 'You don't take a pearl necklace and throw it into a pig pen and expect the pig to put it on and look beautiful, do you?'

Waiting and being patient can be difficult but if you speak to a friend about Jesus and they don't want to listen, you shouldn't just go on and on at them. Wait for the right time. That's being wise.

Lesson Three: Trust God as your Heavenly Father. He will give you everything you really need. Good fathers give their children what they need, don't they? So why not trust the Great and Good Father?

And if you are in his family, you will think: What would I like others to do for me? Then you will go and do the same for them.

Lesson Four: It isn't easy to be a disciple of Jesus. It is like going through a narrow door and walking on a narrow road – when everyone else goes through a broad door and is on a broad road.

So, you need to make a decision. You need to know that Jesus' way is not the easier way. But the narrow road is the only one that leads to life with Jesus.

Lesson Five: Some people pretend to follow Jesus. But they are really only interested in themselves. They want others to do what they say. How can you tell the difference between a true disciple and one who is false?

Watch out for the way they live. Do they love Jesus? Are they humble, like Jesus? Does their teaching help you to love and serve Jesus? Or are they really more interested in themselves?

Jesus helps me to be wise by showing me how his teaching works in my life. He teaches me how to please him and to live for him in a sinful world.

The Bible is full of wisdom. Wisdom is being able to work things out in the best possible way. God is wise – he does everything in the best possible way.

One of the Psalms in the Old Testament tells us that God's teaching can make us even wiser than the old people. It can even make us wiser than our teachers.

Jesus was wise. He thought a lot about God's Word. He loved to see how he could put it into practice. God's Word told Jesus what was really in people's hearts. So he knew how to speak to them.

How do we become wise? We become wise the same way Jesus did.

We read the Bible. We think about what it says. We ask God to help us to do what it says.

Wisdom isn't something you can get in a day. It takes time. But it's worth its weight in gold!

We need wisdom when life is difficult and when everything is going well.

'From infancy you have known the holy Scriptures which are able to make you wise for salvation through faith in Christ Jesus.' 2 Timothy 3:15.

Are you wise? Do you know what God wants from you? Read God's word and ask him what you should do. In the bible in James 1:5 we are told 'If anyone wants wisdom he should ask God for it and it will be given to him.'